THE GAME

BY JANE SIMON

Copyright © by Harcourt Brace & Company

All rights reserved. No part of this publication may be reproduced or transmitted in any form or by any means, electronic or mechanical, including photocopy, recording, or any information storage and retrieval system, without permission in writing from the publisher.

Requests for permission to makes copies of any part of the work should be mailed : Permissions Department, Harcourt Brace & Company, 6277 Sea Harbor Drive, Orlando, FL 32887-6777.

HARCOURT BRACE and Quill Design is a registered trademark of Harcourt Brace & Company.

Printed in the United States of America

ISBN 0-15-313833-5

Ordering Options
ISBN 0-15-313991-9 (Grade 1 Collection)
ISBN 0-15-314042-9 (package of 5)

5 6 7 8 9 175 10 09 08 07

Sam is all by himself again.

He wants to catch and throw.
He wants to play.

Sam is sad.

"Hello, Sam!"
"Come play here!"

"Yes! Now I can play with you!" said Sam. "I'll come over there."

"Will you throw? I want to catch," Sam said.

More animals came by. The game went on and on.

"Now let's eat!" Sam cried.

TAKE-HOME BOOK
Big Dreams
Use with "Later, Rover."